Good Fight

This
Good Fight

Poems by

JOSÉ CHAMBERS

ℂℙ

THE CHOIR PRESS

First published in the United Kingdom in 2019 by
The Choir Press

ISBN 978-1-78963-063-3

This collection of poems grew from
this woman's life –
a life lived in the second half of the 20th century and
these early years of the 21st.

One theme of the collection is the precarious balance between "I"
and "you" – the incessant to-and-fro between the external life,
the life of others, and the life in the head.

The poems were written in an order quite different from the order
in which they appear here.
They are arranged here so that, if you decide to read them from the
beginning, you progress, as it were,
through a life.

Asking myself about the role of poetry in the 21st century,
I look for ways of using language simply and sparingly –
whilst squeezing from few words a richer range of possibilities.

These poems are for you, whoever you are,
but especially for everyone who has been part of my life
and made it worth this good fight.
You know who you are.

JC, February 2019

Contents

I

Living – and partly living

"Living and partly living
Picking together the pieces,
Gathering faggots at nightfall,
Building a partial shelter,
For sleeping and eating and drinking and laughter."

The Chorus of Women in
T.S. Eliot's *Murder in the Cathedral*

"Is there anyone really alive out there?"

A Springsteen trope

Living

Yes.

There are lots of us alive

Out here.

Partly,

At least.

Half-circles

Be a child again,
Hiding.
Clumped redcurrant bushes
Cluster close,
Shadowing your secrets.

Through the leaves a woman
Hangs out bright washing.

Another day, you both stand,
Ankle deep, in river water.
It slides, cold and green,
Pushing silt between your toes.

"Now – let's have our picnic."
You walk back together,
Across a field spiked with thistles.

Here is the place,
Near the old house.
But the redcurrant pie
Is half-eaten –
"The chickens must have found it!"

On its chipped enamel plate,
Pecked, ragged,
Pink as a mouth:

You see it still.

Tangle

I know, now,
That I was four,
When I came
Through the door,
And saw
My father,
Wearing a gas mask:
Hideous green – rubber,
Strapped and goggled.

The war must
Have been over
For years,
Yet here he was,
Monstered,
One Sunday morning,
Before lunch.

My mother and grandmother
Bustled to scold.
He tore off the mask,
Roared back:
They had not seen – as he had –
Men mangled,
Men strewn across hedges.

I remember those phrases.
He seemed to use them often.
For years he slept
Under khaki army blankets.
Ordinary blankets
Were not
Heavy enough.

He carried the war
Home with him,
In his head and his hands.
And I did not understand,
And wished he had been left,
Tangled,
In a hedgerow in France.

From a daughter to a daughter

"Loving," she said,
"Is not sending someone away."
"I want to stay with you
 All day;
 Still, when I am bigger,
 I shall stay."

Loving, I think,
Can be sending someone away.
And you will not
Want to stay.
Then, when you are bigger,
You will go away.

II

Days

7

Breaking fast

Feel an ice cold November day,
The roadway edged with black:
Boughs, bushes, trees –
Tangled, toughened,
Wintering.

Here and there
Apples cling,
Plump balls.
They punctuate the dark-knit mesh:
Red, green, yellow,
Bright globes whispering:
'Reach out to me.
Eat me.
Now.'

Try another day. Feel August:
Early morning orange grove,
Already hot.
Dried grass crunches under foot.
You stroll, searching for stray fruit.
And there they are:
Single oranges, hanging on,
Leftovers –
Leathered skin taut with juice.

Clutching five or six,
You turn back to the house.
Grey-ridged mountains tumble;
Blue sky burns.

In the dark stone kitchen,
You fill two glasses with sun.
Another day begun.

Present words

"Welcome."
"You are always welcome,
Now – or any time."

Some words sing
Like marigolds in blue air;
Some words link hands,
Shine roundly,
Settle gently, like dust.

Welcome these words.
Open your days to them.
Now, or any time.

Ball

Inside the house,
We warm a green melon
In window sun,
Till it strokes like skin,
Sucks like honey.

In the all-green garden
Someone has left
A yellow ball.
It collects the day's light,
Displays it roundly.

With invisible threads,
Some green, some yellow,
We spin word nets:
"Wild tortoises",
"Hot gooseberries."

This is how this day is made,
Threaded, woven, displayed.
We in it
Taste what comes our way,
Collect what sun we may.

Lessons in Watercolour

In the municipal garden
A desultory gardener
Picks away, tidying a border
Crammed with colour.

The advice of our teacher
Is good for watercolours
And for life:
"Concentrate on something
Small
And controllable."

Instructed, we focus:
Mixing colours, naming them;
Flooding one into another,
Watching as they blossom:
Adults, absorbed like children,
As the afternoon park
Slips into an evening
Of soft grey.

Détente Cordiale

"C'est bon détente à Montenon."
(an inhabitant of Montenon confirms the undeniable)

In this high hamlet
Another day slides away
In quiet play.

We are painting;
They are meditating.

She slips the prayer beads
One by one through her fingers,
Then stands
High, on the wall's edge,
Opens her arms to all the day.

I puzzle, testing languidly,
Which blues to use
To catch the dense bright sky?

Down there the trees
Stand in rows,
Packed with purpled plums.

This Good Fight

My next door neighbour
Is cutting down
His apple tree:
Sawn limbs raw, where leaves once were.
"It's got honey fungus."
It's dead now anyway.

On the other side of the hedge,
I battle with buttercups –
Clinging string roots,
Matted and wedged,
Clamped to clay.

Against such insidious invasions
We stay outwardly stalwart,
Buoyed up by spring
With all its loud paraphernalia:
Daffodils, bird song,
The inevitable new green.

The clear air however
Sings a sharp, quite other note:
In this good fight
None of us wins.
Use it then:
Break fences;
Bind wounds;
Join hands.

Still: Life in Winchester

It's autumn, but still Saturday
Picnics on the cathedral green.

Three grey-haired women
Eat their sandwiches
On the warmed stone
Of war memorial steps,
Legs open to the sun.

Above them the soldier stands,
Stalwart in bronze,
Stiff, still young,
But greening.
He grips his gun,
Spikes the air,
Keeps his bayonet
Fixed.

It's 2001. "Our boys"
Are in Afghanistan. Now.

In my Winchester garden
Simple tasks:
Raking leaves,
Picking up walnuts,
Planting bulbs,
Are all underpinned with guilt.

Hot desert sand lodges
In this Hampshire head.

Malvern

The Malvern Hills *"are said to have constituted a portion of the sea-bed of a primeval ocean, after it had become cool, crystallised, consolidated and upheaved to the surface."*

Guide to Malvern, 1924.

We go to the dentist's in Malvern.
Pain is polished;
Decay dressed in white.

In the street sunlight
An old lady
Carries her small shopping bag,
To a house with a turret
And a monkey puzzle tree.
She leans on an ivory handled stick,
Stopping to watch
Bare-kneed boys
From the Busy Bee Preparatory School
Cross the road in twos.

Behind, above, always
The weight of the hills:
Bare, ridged, brown.

The silence of erosion
Fills this gentle, polished town.

On the Beach

The beach is crowded.
We sit in households.

"Do that again and I'll wallop you!"
Sun makes fun of indoor bodies:
Her dimpled thighs are strangely white;
Her calves sinewy, pink.

Shabby pains squirm on the sand,
Like worms left on the surface,
When the rain has stopped.

Life is what you make it?

Sometimes foolish words
Weigh more
Than wise ones.

"Life is like a mantelpiece."

I write this to a friend.
I write it on the back of a postcard.
On the front is a picture:
A mantelpiece,
With a clock, some flowers,
A few objects,
Carefully arranged.

I think she will understand
What I try to hold in words:
Precarious treasures carefully placed;
Jumble of trivia, dust and time,
Beauty underpinned by pain.

Life is what you make it.
Let's make it a mantelpiece
Today.

Cell

When she told them she would try to escape,
The others said:
'At least here is safe, warm, dry.'
'If we wait long enough,
Behave well,
Our time for freedom will come around.'

Nevertheless, she did escape.
And was not brought back.

In the years that followed,
As their walls thickened, grew tall,
They imagined her wanderings.
Huddled together, they
Convinced themselves of her folly.

She, outside, stumbled into new traps,
But she had learned the habits of escape.

So she found, here and there,
Pathways,
Now and then
A clearing;
Often,
Fine threads of sunlight.

III

Sisters

"Standing on their own two feet; ringing their own bells,
Sisters are doing it for themselves."

Annie Lennox and Dave Stewart, The Eurthymics

Plan B

Every woman needs a plan.
Try yours for size:
Ease into it
If you can.

Currently I intend,
About sixty-six or so,
To grow into a mad old thing
Predictably painting watercolours.

I shall buy walking boots
And feathered hats
And probably wear cardigans.
I shall wilfully perplex young men.

(By then
My garden will be heavy
With intricately petalled roses
Planted long ago.)

Every woman needs a plan.
Nourish yours.
Flourish in it,
While you can.

Framed

*(as seen in the 19th Century gallery of the
Museum of Modern Art, Milan)*

All these painted women,
Framed.

The lady with a candle,
The woman in white;
Women with lilies,
"With pompoms" even;
With a lute; at the piano;
Letter writing; letter reading;
Wearing the hat with the blue bow.

Mothers, goddesses,
Daughters, wives,
Sitting clothed, coy, dutiful;
Lying naked, languorous.
Rarely active:
Sometimes tending the sick,
Or grieving the dead;
A dancer maybe,
A whore perhaps.

But look – here – nine nuns,
Pictured "au bord de la mer":
Their head-dresses stiff white sails,
Their long blue gowns flapping.
See them turn to each other, wind-blown –
It's a still life,
But still, a life.

Bird Song in Hong Kong?

Sunday in Hong Kong:
The tight spaces between
High rise towers
Are filling up …

Chattering flocks of women
Cluster, perch,
Cut each other's hair,
Share photographs:
Talking, talking . . . . . .

"Who are they?"
"Why so many?"
"Look – everywhere!"

Maids, cooks, shop girls,
Far from home;
Migrant birds,

Out …

For the day.

If One Should, Accidentally, Fall

Last night, round a fire,
We three, women, conjured truth
From three green bottles,
Stayed awake for each other,
Kept our cauldron bubbling.

Now, a new day's sun dances in
Through window hung with ice:
Lays out a warm coffin shape –
Tempting, confining, precise.

This woman's body chooses life,
Refuses languor,
Pushes aside the wine-frost head,
Decides to keep the frogs jumping.

If one should, accidentally, fall,

It doesn't have to matter – at all.

Two beds

She was there, she said,
To have a stitch in her womb
To save her second child.

She was twenty-two.
Her husband
Knocked her about, she said.
He had another woman.

She said she didn't
Want this child,
But the doctors
Wouldn't "help her."

Her stark weary eyes
Rarely met mine.
But I watched her then
And I think of her now.

I was the woman in the bed opposite.
I was "the lady who reads *The Times*."
(Actually I asked
For *The Guardian*.)

Eating out, alone and delighted

*(At a restaurant table in the Place du Malby,
Bordeaux, on a hot August evening)*

In his yellow shirt
He walks the top floor, throws
Open his shutters.

Now he seasons the night air:
Sends us a Beethoven
String Quartet:

Strings sing through the square,
Sharp, yielding:
Tasting of *framboises au sucre.*

View from the Desk

(A teacher's poem from the 1980s)

There they sit, the boys, energy simmering;
With their Puma bags and their big boots,
Cropped hair and maybe an ear-ring,
Eyes grinning, sprawling awkward at tables,
Waiting to kick and run.
They spread their books across the desk:
But these are trimmings from a stranger's world.

There they sit, the girls, already shaping
Nests of neatness, dutiful, acquiescent;
Pencil cases, paper, arranged with pleased carefulness,
Chosen, as they may choose cups and curtains,
To feather out their submissiveness.

And here I sit, in the middle.

Listen

We have been grouped
To hear you speak.

Outside,
Cedar branches spread and sway,
Lifting like fingers,
Beckoning.

Again, again, wind swings
Through needled green.
Rain threads, stiff, insistent,
Soaks bark dark,
Shines it here, there.

I choose to ignore you.

The wind and the rain speak to me.

I decide,
Arrogantly, no doubt,
That you
Do not.

IV

On the other hand

"i carry your heart with me (i carry it in my heart)"

e.e.cummings

"Real world?"

For me,
Increasingly,
"Real world' is a conjuring,
A fantasy,
A coining – it says:
"Beware."

"Real world"
Hovers,
Over there,
Beyond reach;
Lurks under everyday skins,
Seldom breaks through.

You though,
With your challenge,
Your rare smile, your you,
Bring me the moment –
Present me with here,
So that this, for now at least,

Seems real.

On the one hand

Sisters,
I apologise
For all those eyes
And smiles of yours
I did not prize.

You see
I was tricked, by history,
And thought that men
Stand at the centre
Of this mystery.

On the other hand,

Mingling
Seems true,
Merely sitting
Next to you. Strange exchange
Shimmering between us,
Telling me to stay,
Lay my head
On your shoulder,
Lie in your lap.

I've had this dream before.
But I still want more.

This love

This love arrives whole:
Pre-assembled,
Most bridges built,
Rainbows at the ready.

It is seamless,
Made-to-measure,
Sets us walking,
Allows room for growth.

It locates treasure easily:
Arched windows; a peacock;
Wind-blown sky; green hollows;
Warm black rock.

It sidles in, crab-quiet,
And in disguise.
Now it sits here,
Squarely,

Like a fact.

London Eye

You

Lift me up:

Bright white greeting,

Round hallo,

See through

Tambourine.

Toronto ice

Two in the morning,
In the crisped city square,
And they're still playing ice hockey,
Silently.

Sliding shunt;
Knock of sticks;
Slurred scrunch of blades:
Silence settles
On their breathing,
A focussed, earnest mist.

And you and I
Straight from our taxi,
Fresh from that party
(In a snow-bright house
By a lake we didn't see):

Far from home
But at home,
Warming
To this icy welcome.

Table talk

"I am here," he says.
And I am filled with wonder.
(In this the Chablis
Plays no part.)

"I feel sad," he says.
And I am filled with gloom.
(But still the waiter smiles,
And wears an ear-ring.)

"I need you," I fail to say.
Nonetheless, I think he hears,
As he sits, sifting, sorting,
Through his pile of moules.

"You make me happy," he says,
Wearing the dark blue shirt.
And unaccountably I know this
To be true.

Not a poem about Tuscany

"There are no poems about Tuscany," you say.

"No," I reply and wonder why.
Perhaps it's no longer possible
To write about Tuscany?

The idyll is too well-tried,
The images freeze-dried.
Perfection poses problems.

Still, I remember the bathrooms:
Terracotta floors slowly shedding footprints;
White tiles, icy; wood beams, adze-hewn.

Then you, waiting:
Rough grain of cotton sheets;
Backcloth of hills and sun.

The most vivid Tuscan memory is you;
What being with you can be like:
What we can become when simply happy.

"Troppo Silenzio?"

Geraniums everywhere;
Horizon edged by black cypresses.

Sun sliding through silk water,
Hockney-coloured pool.

Some kind of perfection;
Some kind of dream.

A church bell rings across the valley;
An occasional dog barks.

"Troppo silenzio?"
Enquires our host.

In the garden below
Two Italians pick tomatoes.

"I forgive you."

You said it first.
We two too new
To guess the years
That stretched ahead.
My sin? Arriving late.
"I didn't expect the snow;
Didn't know how far."

I also did not know,
Then,
How time matters.

Those who already knew you,
However, knew only too well:
"She was 45 minutes late
And I forgave her!"
A circle of laughter,
Shared zest,
Momentum.

Twenty-five years on,
The themes remain;
The pleasures hold.
I forgive you too,
Knowing that there
Is, in truth,
Nothing to forgive.

Making it

What do I want?
What do you want?
What do we want?

What do we want to make happen?
What do we really need to make happen?

Always our questions
Shape the answer.

Behind every question
The answer can be

"Yes".

Yes,
It is possible

To make things different.

And to make them differently.

V

"Who comes so fast in silence of the night?"

Lorenzo in Shakespeare's *The Merchant of Venice*

In Transit

Briefly,
And by chance,
We are in transit:
Displaced;
Onlookers;
Eyes sharpened
By the unfamiliar.

Briefly,
And by choice,
We are at home:
Rooted;
Players;
Eyes blurred
By the known.

But seldom,
If ever,
By choice
Or by chance,
Do we savour,
The brevity
Of our stay.

Home from the Vet

"It is a kindness
to be able to do that",
He says,
Handing me my dead cat.

We knew each other,
Cat and I,
For twenty years.

I knew him chiefly
By his weight and his warmth,
Settled by my side at night,
"Better than a man."

And by his greetings:
Small morning sounds,
The lifting of his head;
Routines, expectations,
Claws.

So I pause,
In tears,
As I drive him,
Carefully,
Home.

We are the Leaf Peepers

In New England,
We ageing ones are out catching autumn.
Snatching late gold,
Watching and waiting.
Not working any more,
Slowly mellowing instead,
Wrapped in fleece; warmed by quilted coats.

All round us the hills are quilted too:
Cushioned in yellow, red, lingering green.
Trees greet us with lightly lifting hands.
Our heads tell a bleaker dying tale:
Thinned hair, greying, white,
Or slashed with shouts of colour.

Like the leaves, we are all
Slowly loosening our grip:
Shrugging a painful shoulder,
Flexing a replaced hip.
We peep through failing eyes,
Try out a few tentative goodbyes.

Boxed

Inside the bone
Of your own
Skull
Always,
All days, sings
A song of self.

He said
He dreamed
His skull was
Boxed
And on a shelf.

His self looked out
And saw the others,
Staring in.

They did not know
He was still there
And had not gone away
That day
His body
Decided

To betray him.

House

Once my house
Had a dark corridor
Upstairs.
It went down some steps
And round a corner.

Once it shivered me
To think
What waited there
To catch me
Unawares.

Now, more and more,
I know there is nothing
Waiting, after all,
Just emptiness,
Beckoning.

The Child

I carry my death inside me.
Occasional stirrings, slight quivers,
Have trembled me on bright hot days
When even rhubarb leaves lie limp
And cut worms eat the bean plants,
But I have forced my fork more fiercely
Into the soil and sprayed the greenfly.

Now, locked in winter,
Wrapped in grey sheets:
Ice, fog, frost, snow,
I feel this death child kick my ribs.

Soon I will turn over in bed
And let him come.

To my friends – whoever they are

"I think –
It seems to me –
That there is evasion enough.

And I would like
To have done with it ….
I think."

Even as I say this,
I hide meaning behind word masks.
My hands make shapes in the air.

Perhaps the meaning rests
There,
Somewhere,

In the space between us.

Whoever you are,
Know I need you;
Whatever that means.

I Sight

Let's look at it this way:
The only eye, really,
Is the I
In your own head.

But sometimes an other's
Eye sheds some light,
Gleams in the night,
Shifts the seen.

And that rare glimmer –
The swift, tricky glimpse
Of the you
That others see
Opens up a new view.

Suddenly the light
Gets through:
Then 'just me'
Becomes me
And you –
Us.

Notes

Tangle

My father was a gentle and sensitive man. He joined the Grenadier Guards in 1936, when he was 19 and working as a blacksmith's striker. He was determined to escape being a miner in the Staffordshire coalmines, like his father. He would tell the story of how, before the war, based at Chelsea Barracks, he had to travel on the underground, with his bearskin on his lap, off 'to guard the Bank of England'. He served in the Grenadier Guards throughout the Second World War. In 1941, his regiment spent days on the beaches at Dunkirk guarding the perimeter. A non-swimmer (no seaside holidays and no nearby swimming pools when he was a child), he eventually managed to escape from the beaches by wading out to a Dutch flat-bottomed boat. Once back in the UK he was sent to Salisbury Plain to be re-trained as a tank driver. He returned to Europe in the Guards Armoured Division, driving his tank into Brussels as part of the liberation of Belgium.

Boxed

Years ago, with friends, I visited churches in Brittany. In the church porches, wooden boxes – each containing a skull – were mounted on the wall in rows. Each skull stared out at the onlooker through a small hole in the front of the box. Years later one of those friends, who had since suffered a severe stroke, shared this dream.

We are the Leaf Peepers
Visitors to the New England autumn scene are known locally as 'leaf peepers'.

Bird Song in Hong Kong and Cell
These poems were recently published in *Mingled Verses – International Prize Anthology* – Proverse, Hong Kong.

[Originally an English teacher, chance encounters later took José Chambers into the fields of professional and organisational learning, working mainly with the public sector. Retiring from the role of Assistant Vice Chancellor of the University of Winchester in 2011, she was awarded the MBE for services to Higher Education. She now co-ordinates work funded by the Comino Foundation, an educational charity.]